Paul de Keyser

Violin Study Time

A second book of studies for the young violinist

FABER *ff* MUSIC

© 1988 by Faber Music Ltd
First published in 1988 by Faber Music Ltd
Bloomsbury House, 74–77 Great Russell Street, London WC1B 3DA
Music set by Musicpage Ltd
Cover illustration © Penny Dann
Cover design by M & S Tucker
Printed in England

ISBN10: 0-571-51014-0
EAN13: 978-0-571-51014-6

To buy Faber Music publications or to find out about the full range of titles available
please contact your local music retailer or Faber Music sales enquiries:

Faber Music Limited, Burnt Mill, Elizabeth Way, Harlow, CM20 2HX England
Tel: +44 (0)1279 82 89 82   Fax: +44 (0)1279 82 89 83
sales@fabermusic.com   fabermusicstore.com

VIOLIN STUDY TIME

In the vast literature for the violin, studies lie midway between exercises and repertoire pieces, encouraging the development of a sound technique. A good study focuses on one particular technical point, while at the same time maintaining melodic and musical interest.

Violin Study Time is a second anthology of established and newly composed studies that develops the young violinist's technique in several directions. It may be used in conjunction with the *Young Violinist's Repertoire* series. There are studies for various types of bowing such as *détaché* and *spiccato*, studies for finger action and basic shifts, and several studies that introduce third position.

I hope that these studies will serve as an introduction to the great repertoire of violin studies, so that before long the young violinist will be tackling the works of Kreutzer, Rode, Dont, and even Wieniawski and Paganini!

Paul de Keyser

CONTENTS

Part I

1.	For Velocity *Carl Czerny*	page 1
2.	Triplets *Bartolomeo Campagnoli*	1
3.	Carneval de Venise *Jacques-Féréol Mazas*	1
4.	Galloping *Campagnoli*	2
5.	Mazurka *Franz Wohlfahrt*	2
6.	Triplets *Charles Dancla*	2
7-8.	Two Spiccato Studies *Ottokar Ševčík*	3
9.	Bariolage *Dancla*	4
10.	Polka *Wohlfahrt*	4
11.	Study in 3rd Position *Charles de Bériot*	5
12.	First-Finger Fantasy	5
13.	Irish Song	5
14.	Andante in E minor *Ševčík*	6
15.	Theme and Variations *de Bériot*	6

Part II

16.	Détaché *Ševčík, arr. P. de K.*	8
17.	Finger Agility *H. Schradieck*	8
18.	3rd-Position Study *Wohlfahrt, arr. P. de K.*	9
19.	Allegro *Ferdinand Küchler*	9
20.	Skater's Waltz *Wohlfahrt, arr. P. de K.*	10
21.	3rd-Position Study	10
22.	3rd-Position Study *Dancla arr. P. de K.*	11
23.	Folk Dance *Milanova*	11
24.	Study in F *Dancla*	12
25.	Allegro Moderato *Wohlfahrt*	12
26.	3rd-Position Study *Joseph Joachim*	13
27.	Accidentals in 3rd Position *Wohlfahrt*	13
28-29.	Two Studies for building Arpeggios *Dancla, arr. P. de K.*	14
30.	A la Valse *Ševčík*	15

Violin Study Time Part I

1. For Velocity

Carl Czerny
(1791-1857)

2. Triplets

Bartolomeo Campagnoli
(1751-1827)

3. Carneval de Venise

Jacques-Féréol Mazas
(1782-1849)

4. Galloping

Campagnoli

5. Mazurka

Franz Wohlfahrt
(1833-1884)

Tempo di mazurka

6. Triplets

Charles Dancla
(1817-1907)
arr. P. de K.

❋The use of the number 5 denoting 4th finger extensions is a convention which helps to establish the principle that only the little finger moves, the wrist, hand and other fingers remaining absolutely still.

Two Spiccato Studies
7.

Ottokar Ševčík
(1852-1934)
arr. P. de K.

8.

4

9. Bariolage

Dancla

Moderato

10. Polka

Wohlfahrt

Allegro

11. Study in 3rd Position

Charles de Bériot
(1802-1870)

12. First-Finger Fantasy

13. Irish Song

6

14. Andante in E minor

Ševčík

15. Theme and Variations

de Bériot

Variation II

Variation III

Part II
16. Détaché

Ševčík, arr. P. de K.

17. Finger Agility

H. Schradieck
(1846-1918)

18. 3rd-Position Study

Wohlfahrt, arr. P. de K.

19. Allegro

Ferdinand Küchler
(1857-?)

From the *Concertino in the style of Vivaldi*, Op. 15.
Printed by kind permission of Bosworth & Co.

20. Skaters' Waltz

Wohlfahrt, arr. P. de K.

21. 3rd-Position Study

22. 3rd-Position Study

Dancla, arr. P. de K.

23. Folk Dance

Milanova

24. Study in F

Dancla

25. Allegro moderato

Wohlfahrt

26. 3rd-Position Study

27. Accidentals in 3rd Position

28. Two Studies for Building Arpeggios

Dancla, arr. P. de K.

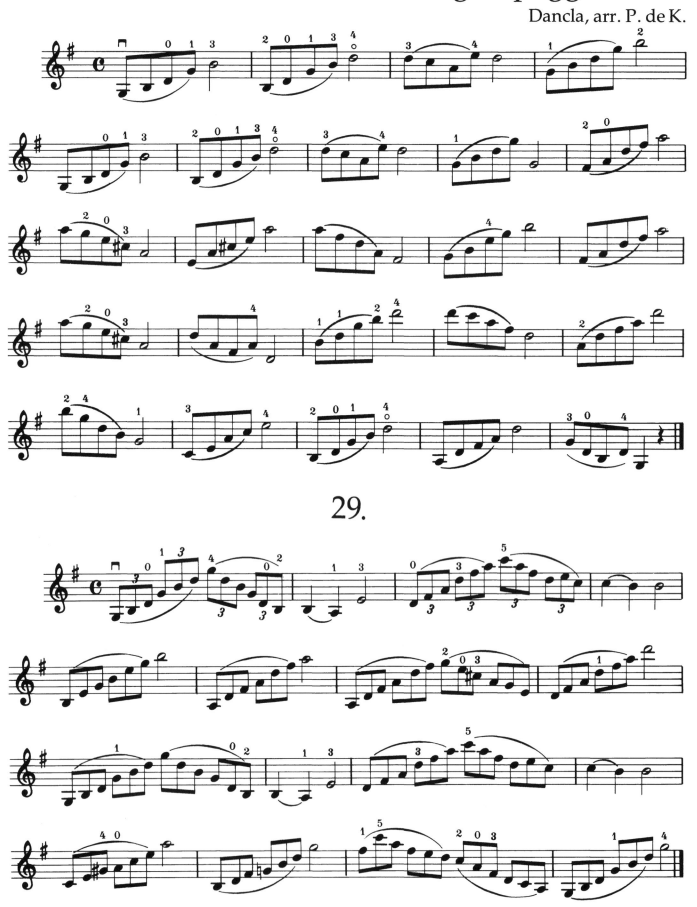

29.

30.   A la Valse

Ševčík

REPERTOIRE BOOKS FOR YOUNG VIOLINISTS

The Young Violinist's Early Music Collection (Grades 1–5)

Ten gems for violin and piano
arranged by Edward Huws Jones

Brawls, galliards, and madrigals: make a
fascinating journey into the past with this
stylish repertoire collection from France, Italy,
Spain and Britain.

This brilliant selection of ancient pieces is
arranged by Edward Huws Jones for
intermediate-level violin with simple piano
accompaniment.

Who says early music is boring!?

The Young Violinist's Early Music Collection   ISBN 0-571-51669-6

Up-Grade!

Light relief between grades
by Pamela Wedgwood

Tired of the same old exam pieces? Looking for
something to bridge the gap between grades?
Need a bit of light relief? *Up-Grade!* is for you!

Pam Wedgwood's inimitable style is
guaranteed to breathe new life into your violin
playing – the varied pieces and duets in these
bright collections range from toe-tapping jazzy
numbers to more classical styles, all designed
to ease you gently on towards the next grade.

So lighten up and move on with *Up-Grade!*

Up-Grade! Violin Grades 1–2 ISBN 0-571-51954-7
Up-Grade! Violin Grades 2–3 ISBN 0-571-51955-5